Lumberjacks

by Ann Parrott

illustrated by Burgandy Beam

Editorial Offices: Glenview, Illinois • Parsippany, New Jersey • New York, New York
Sales Offices: Needham, Massachusetts • Duluth, Georgia • Glenview, Illinois
Coppell, Texas • Ontario, California • Mesa, Arizona

Every effort has been made to secure permission and provide appropriate credit for photographic material. The publisher deeply regrets any omission and pledges to correct errors called to its attention in subsequent editions.

Unless otherwise acknowledged, all photographs are the property of Scott Foresman, a division of Pearson Education.

Illustrations by Burgandy Beam

ISBN: 0-328-13436-8

4 5 6 7 8 9 10 V0G1 14 13 12 11 10 09 08 07 06

Paul Bunyan: Lumberjack

Old stories say that Paul Bunyan was a giant lumberjack, or logger. When he was born, his father used five trees to make his cradle. As he grew, Paul needed a lot to eat. His hotcakes were cooked on a huge griddle. Men greased it using bacon as skates! Paul grew so big that his footprints filled with water and became lakes.

Paul's pet, Babe the Blue Ox, was huge too. The space between Babe's eyes was longer than forty-two axe handles.

Of course, Paul Bunyan was not a real man. But loggers in the United States in the 1800s were strong and tough workers. They liked to brag about their strength and to tell tall tales about heroes like Paul Bunyan. Their stories made workdays pass quickly.

The Discovery of Gold and Other Treasure

The cry of "Gold!" brought thousands of people west to California around 1849. All these people needed homes, and lumber was needed to build these homes. There was lots of work for lumberjacks.

Soon lumberjacks heard of another kind of "treasure" farther north. According to the stories, there were huge trees in **immense** forests. Some of the biggest trees are called redwoods. Many lumberjacks headed north to find the big trees.

At an Early Logging Camp

After lumberjacks found an area good for logging, they built a logging camp. The men lived there for months while they cut logs. A logger's shanty, or house, was not fancy. It had a big fireplace in the middle for cooking and heating. A hole in the roof let out the smoke.

Loggers slept on bunks with straw mattresses. They kept all their belongings near their bunks. Loggers even sat on their bunks to eat.

The inside of a logger's shanty might have looked like this.

The lumberjacks needed to eat a lot of food because they worked so hard. Their breakfast might have included oatmeal, prunes, pork and beans on toast, raisin pie, cheese, and bread and butter. Hot tea always finished a meal.

Lumberjacks carried their lunches—maybe pork and cheese sandwiches—out to their work site in the forest. They usually ate two lunches, one at 9:00 A.M. and the other at 1:00 P.M. The cook often served supper around 7:00 P.M. Supper might have included pea soup, beef, pork and mustard, sugar pie, raisin pie, molasses cookies, cheese, bread and butter, milk, and, of course, hot tea.

The rule at some logging camps was "No talking. Eat quickly."

The first step in lumbering was to chop down a tree. This is not too difficult with a small tree, but the redwood trees of California are huge. They can be fifteen feet wide near their base. Loggers started by building a platform a few feet off the ground. The tree was not as thick there. They stood on the platform to chop down the tree. It took a two-man team several days to cut down a large redwood. These men had to plan carefully to do the work safely. They also had to watch out for dangerous animals, such as **grizzly** bears.

Once a tree was chopped down, the loggers had to move it out of the forest to a sawmill. Then the tree was cut into lumber. To get ready for the move, lumberjacks cut off branches and bark. Then they used horse or oxen teams and their own strength to roll the logs down to a rough road.

The road, called a "skid road," was made of logs laid a few feet apart. These logs, or skids, were partly pressed into the ground. Horses or oxen pulled the cut logs across the skids. Loggers would grease the skids with oil or water. This made the cut logs slide easily.

This skid road was so slippery with ice that just two horses could pull all these logs.

Down to the River

The logs were pulled to a nearby river. The lumberjacks built a dam in the river to collect the logs. Once the river was full of logs, it was time to send them downstream to a sawmill. This was dangerous. Often the logs were jammed so tightly in the river that a dynamite blast was needed to start the logs on their trip.

As the logs moved, loggers climbed on top to guide them. If a logger fell, he could easily be hurt or even killed by the heavy logs. Loggers were eager to reach the sawmill. That was where the **payroll** was worked out so the loggers could get paid.

At the Sawmill

Water did most of the work at sawmills. The force of the rushing water turned a waterwheel. The turning waterwheel powered the saws that cut the logs.

With a loud roar, saws cut planks from the logs. Sawdust filled the air. Men carried the planks to big tables. Then they sorted them by size. Next, they piled the planks beside the mill in a lumberyard.

Improvements in the Process

A steam-powered engine called a donkey was made to move logs from the forest to the river. One kind of donkey engine was built by a man who used to work on ships. He changed a ship's lifting device to make it work in the woods.

Later, loggers began using railroads to get logs to a sawmill. Lumberjacks no longer had to ride their logs down the river to the sawmill. Donkey engines loaded logs onto railway cars to be taken to the sawmill.

Strong bridges were built to carry train tracks across valleys. To everyone's **dismay,** trains sometimes fell from the tall bridges.

Pulling heavy logs took a lot of power.

Whistle Signals

Logging railroad whistles sent messages. Each whistle had a special meaning:

Short whistle: Stop.

Two long whistles: Go.

Three short whistles: Back up.

Two long and two short whistles: Train crossing highway.

Eight long whistles: Train coming into a station.

Many short whistles: Warning! A person or animal on the track.

Railroad inspectors like this one checked on safety.

Native Americans' Use of Forests

Long before the loggers came to cut down trees, Native Americans lived in the woods and used the resources of the forest.

Native Americans used all parts of the tree. They made harpoons, axe handles, and fish net poles from tree branches. They wove baskets from small tree roots. Tree needles were used to make tea. The trees also provided shelter.

Lumberjacks later used this forest for the logging industry.

Native American redwood bark house

Modern-Day Logging

The newest machine in the logging industry is the skyhook, a helicopter with a long metal cable hanging from it. Cut trees can be attached to the cable. A skyhook can lift many cords of wood, up to eleven thousand pounds! A **cord** of wood is a pile four feet wide, four feet high, and eight feet long.

Even today, lumberjacks work hard in forests across the United States. Some of them still like to retell the old Paul Bunyan stories to pass their time!

Glossary

cord *n.* a measure of quantity for cut wood, equal to 128 cubic feet; a pile of wood four feet wide, four feet high, and eight feet long.

dismay *n.* sudden, helpless fear of what is about to happen or what has happened.

grizzly *n.* grizzly bear; a large, gray or brownish-gray bear of western North America.

immense *adj.* very large; huge; vast.

payroll *n.* a list of persons to be paid and the amount that each one is to receive.